D0427293

The Paranoid's Pocket Guide

ARE YOU SURE THIS IS DECAF?

[A CUP OF COFFEE]

Copyright © 1997 by Chronicle Books
Photographs copyright © 1997 by Anthony
Pardines

All rights reserved. No part of this book may be reproduced in
any form without written permission from the publisher.

Library of Congress Cataloging-in-Publication Data.

    Tuttle, Cameron.
        The paranoid's pocket guide /
      by Cameron Tuttle.
          p.   cm.
        ISBN 0-8118-1665-6
        1. Paranoia-Humor.
        I. Title   PN6231. P16T88
        1997   96-37545
        818'. 5407--dc21 CIP

Printed in the United States of America.

Research assistants: Julien Gorbach and Daniel Spiro

Book design: Martine Trélaün

Distributed in Canada by Raincoast Books
8680 Cambie Street
Vancouver, B.C. V6P 6M9

10 9 8 7 6 5 4 3

Chronicle Books
85 Second Street
San Francisco, CA 94105

Web Site: www.chronbooks.com

THE
PARANOID'S
Pocket Guide

Cameron Tuttle

Photographs by Anthony Pardines

CHRONICLE BOOKS
SAN FRANCISCO

I used to think I was crazy because I worried all the time about the most ridiculous things. (Is it just a coincidence that *paranoia* is right next to *paranormal* in the dictionary? I don't think so.) But then I started to research this book and talk to other people. Now I realize that I haven't been worrying nearly enough.

There are so many marvelous things to obsess over—loss of privacy, new diseases, technological dangers, dating, the environment, life on Mars—it's hard to know where to begin. So I've highlighted sections to help you worry more efficiently: fears about work, home, food, airplanes, driving, and more. "Hypochondriac's Alert" links symptoms you probably have to possible and even horrible medical explanations. "Fabulous Phobias" lists old favorites as well as emerging phobias. Popping up everywhere—and marked with a special warning—are "Fright Bites," shocking yet true statistics and facts. Photographs of seemingly harmless items help warn you about other hidden risks. And running across the bottom of every page you'll find revealing intimate fears that people disclosed to me during my research.

If you're not paranoid about something, you will be after reading this book. (Is this printed on acid-free paper? Is someone reading over your shoulder? Will your purchase of this book be added to a computer profile of you?) You might want to keep this handy guide with you at all times since you never know when you'll get stuck in traffic or trapped in an elevator. For best results, enjoy *The Paranoid's Pocket Guide* late at night, with a flashlight under the covers, alone. And remember, just because you're paranoid doesn't mean that someone isn't out to get you.

FRIGHT 🐔 BITE!

One in 6,500 Americans will be injured by a toilet seat during their lifetime. Most will be men.

Who else has the keys to your car?

A remote keyless entry device lets you unlock your car door at a distance with the click of a button, but someone with a receiver can pick up the signal your keyless remote sends, record it, and resend it later to unlock your car.

Some 3.7 million Americans claim to have been abducted by aliens. Most found it a positive experience.

Why haven't you been contacted?

FRIGHT BITE!

If you sneeze too hard, you can fracture a rib. If you try to suppress a sneeze, you can rupture a blood vessel in your head or neck and die.

I have a hole in my pocket and my money and keys will fall out. People will think

Bottled
at the
source—
of what?

Nearly a third of all bottled drinking water purchased in the United States is contaminated with bacteria.

FRIGHT 🐦 BITE!

One in six adults has agreed to sex because they were just too embarrassed to say no.

I'm a tourist. The glue on envelopes is spreading a fatal disease. My neighbors

CHEMICAL PEELS AND NASAL SAWS

(Excerpted from the program of a recent World Congress on Cosmetic Surgical Rejuvenation of the Face, Body, and Extremities, held in Fort Lauderdale, Florida.)

FRIDAY

11:30 a.m.
"Use of Cheek Neck Flap in Facial Plastic Surgery"

11:45 a.m.
"Removal of Eyeliner Pigmentation with an Argon Laser"

1:30 p.m.
"An Alternative Method for the Nasal Osteotomy Utilizing the Dual Plane Reciprocating Nasal Saw Blade"

2:15 p.m.
Workshop: "How to Prevent a Lawsuit"

6:00 p.m.
Cocktail Party, Grand Ballroom

hear everything that goes on in my bathroom. If I pluck a hair, it will grow back

Good news, bad news. Women are more than twice as likely to climax during intercourse if their partner has extremely symmetrical features. Men with extremely symmetrical features are less attentive to their partners and more inclined to cheat on them.

[SYMMETRICAL FEATURES]

A new genera-tion of germs.

Deadly new germs are emerging around the world at a startling rate. *Equine morbilli* virus, which causes a potentially fatal respiratory illness, was discovered in Australia in 1994; blood banks do not yet screen for recently discovered hepatitis G.; and *Bartonella*, a bacteria discovered in 1990, can cause illnesses ranging from cat scratch fever to fatal heart-valve infections. Humans are exposed to this germ from cats carrying infected fleas. Medical researchers are baffled and expect to see many more unknown mysterious diseases.

by mistake. The dry cleaner smells my clothes. I'll spit out my gum in a winning

Only a few years ago, cooking hamburgers at 140 degrees Fahrenheit was enough to kill most harmful bacteria in the meat. But now burgers must be cooked at 155 degrees for at least 15 seconds to destroy *Escherichia coli* O157:H7, an emerging, deadly strain of bacteria.

Make mine well done.

FRIGHT 🦔 BITE!

Each year, you face a 1 in 13 chance of suffering an accident in your home serious enough to require medical attention.

A Harvard Medical School study suggests that women who drink at least two cups of coffee a day are less likely to commit suicide or get into fatal automobile accidents. Other studies indicate that **CAFFEINE** impairs a woman's fertility.

Live longer, childless.

lottery ticket. I'll arrive at the airport two hours before my flight on the wrong

PANIC DISORDER
INFORMATION
HOTLINE

Are you suffering an
ANXIETY ATTACK?
If so,
CALL
1-(800)-64-PANIC

to reach a toll-free hotline.
Operators are standing by
on weekdays between
9:00 a.m. and 9:00 p.m.
Eastern time. At other
times, feel free to leave a
message and someone will
call you back on the next
business day.

day. If I swallow a watermelon seed, a watermelon will grow in my stomach. I'll

While a person's happiness fluctu- ates, everyone has a naturally set level for happiness— much like body weight. So if you're generally an un- happy person, get used to it.

Some things never change.

FRIGHT 🦔 BITE!

Draw-strings are a leading cause of fashion-related injuries.

call in sick and run into my boss at a movie. I won't be able to remember to

Cheer-leading—now a hazardous contact sport.

Last year, nearly 16,000 cheerleaders required emergency-room treatment for injuries, including sprains, torn knee ligaments, skull fractures, and even paralysis. One of the most dangerous routines—***the Human Pyramid***—has been banned in North Dakota and Minnesota schools.

whom I lied and to whom I told the truth. I'll call a teacher "Mom" in front of

FRIGHT 🐦 BITE!

By the year 2010, each person is expected to generate 1,774 pounds of solid waste per year.

Spontaneous human combustion is most likely to happen during a period of strong magnetic disturbance. No one knows how or why a person seemingly ignites without any external fuel, leaving behind little more than a heap of ashes, an uncharred limb, and a pungent blue smoke hanging in the air, but many victims were wearing slippers at the time.

When was the last time you talked to Grampa?

the whole class. I'll buy 6,000 AAA batteries at a warehouse club just because

IS YOUR SON-IN-LAW REALLY DUCK HUNTING THIS WEEKEND?

There are paramilitary training sites for militia groups and private armies in 23 states.

MAIL-ORDER MADNESS.

In May 1995, an Aryan Nation member living in Ohio was arrested for buying three vials of frozen bubonic plague bacteria through the mail. Federal agents searched his house and found detonating fuses, hand-grenade triggers, and homemade explosive devices.

WHERE IS IT NOW?

In one year, over a ton of explosives, including dynamite, C-4 plastic explosives, ANFO, raw ammonium nitrate, and blasting caps has disappeared from commercial sites in Georgia, California, Oklahoma, Idaho, and Indiana.

Militias

GUNS DON'T KILL PEOPLE, PEOPLE DO.

Weapons recently recovered from antigovernment extremist groups:

1. AK-47
2. M-16
3. AR-15
4. Uzi and SKS assault rifles
5. 9-mm machine guns
6. .50-caliber rifles
7. fully-automatic Mac-10 pistols
8. handguns
9. sawed-off shotguns
10. knives
11. assault rifles with bayonets
12. freeze-dried bubonic plague bacteria
13. ricin, a biological poison
14. grenade launchers
15. dynamite and pipe bombs
16. blasting caps and detonators
17. silencers
18. machine gun and rifle components
19. automatic weapon conversion kits
20. armor-piercing ammunition
21. night-vision binoculars
22. body armor and gas masks
23. gas grenades and plastic handcuffs.

How's the water? Nearly a quarter of all lead exposure comes from drinking water. A toxic metal, lead can cause serious health hazards and even brain damage. The Environmental Protection Agency revealed that over 10% of the U.S. population relies on water systems with unsafe levels of lead. The EPA carefully explained it would be wrong to assume that 30 million people always drink unsafe water; instead, 30 million people drink from sources that are unsafe from time to time. Outmoded pipes in older homes or apartment buildings pose an even higher risk of introducing lead into the water that runs through them.

they are such a bargain. I unintentionally put something in my pocket and will

[A GLASS OF WATER]

Lightning. Lightning is a massive buildup of static electricity. Seconds before you are struck by lightning, all of the hair on your head will stand straight up. Lightning kills approximately 300 Americans every year— more than any other type of natural disaster. Most lightning deaths occur during the summer, when people spend more time outdoors. Lightning tends to strike the most conspicuous person or object in a group; golfers are often struck while holding a metal pin or swinging a club.

be arrested for shoplifting. I won't notice until after lunch that I'm wearing two

Sulfur-based preservatives used legally to enhance the colors and crispness of certain vegetables found in salad bars can cause life-threatening allergic reactions.

Salad bars.

FRIGHT 🗯 BITE!

About 65% of new marriages will end in either divorce or separation.

Video surveillance. How long has that pencil sharpener been in the conference room, and why doesn't it work? Why are there two smoke detectors in the employee lounge? It could be because there is a tiny surveillance camera inside. An alarmingly high number of employers today are spying on their workers with mini video cameras no bigger than a human eyeball. This year alone, more than $2 billion will be spent on closed-circuit video equipment. Companies claim to be monitoring worker productivity, industrial espionage, personal security, or suspected drug use, but they can **see and hear everything**. The next time you look at a light switch, room thermostat, or exit sign, be sure to smile.

feel sorry for me. The toilet-paper roll will be empty. I'll be pushed in front of a

[A SURVEILLANCE CAMERA]

IT'S DANGEROUS JUST
SHOWING UP.

Over two million physical assaults and 7,000 homicides occur in the workplace each year. Homicide is now the leading cause of death for women in the workplace and the second-leading cause of death for men. The typical workplace murderer is a male loner who feels frustrated by problems at work and has few relationships away from his job. The chance of employee violence increases dramatically in a work environment where managers exert too much control and remove individuals' sense of dignity, as well as where workers are encouraged to stifle their anger and frustration, act like team players, and adopt a "can-do" attitude.

DELETED MEMO.

Remember those hostile memos you wrote to vent at your boss and then deleted? They're still in the computer system—along with your cover letter to the headhunter, that screenplay you've been working on during office hours, and all of the other files you think you've destroyed. The chances are very good that your company will hire a data-retrieval expert to resurrect files that employees have deleted. That is, if it hasn't done so already.

BECAUSE THEY'RE PAYING.

Who would ever find out that the appendectomy you had last spring was really liposuction? Your boss. If your employer pays for your medical insurance, your employer can require insurance companies to provide a copy of all your medical records.

KEYSTROKES.

While making personal calls or reading a magazine at the office, you may want to hit the "caps lock" button or another key over and over again. Employers can now monitor your computer and count the number of keystrokes entered per hour.

RETIRED SAVINGS.

Are you sure the money that your employer takes out of your paycheck for retirement is really being deposited in your 401(k)? Then why did the federal government offer a six-month amnesty program in 1996 to companies that "borrowed" money from workers' retirement savings accounts?

JOB INSECURITY.
An adult has a 1 in 33 chance of losing his or her job during the next year.

UNEMPLOYMENT KILLS.
If you are laid off or fired, your worries may soon be over. Death rates are significantly higher among the unemployed.

DIGITAL SURVEILLANCE.
Does your personal password give you a sense of security? That may be all it's doing. Any MIS person can override a password and access your files. One in five companies secretly review employees' computer files, e-mail, or voice mail—and the number is higher for companies with over 1,000 employees. Not only is it technically feasible for your boss to spy on you—it's legal.

Who rings twice?

If you answer the telephone and the caller immediately hangs up, it could just be a wrong number. Or it could be your partner's lover. Do you dare press ***69**, which automatically calls back the last number that called you? (Service available in some areas.)

FRIGHT 🦜 BITE!

Rats multiply so quickly that in 18 months two rats could have over a million descendents.

CONSPIRACY

Theories

1. The eye above the pyramid on the back of a U.S. one dollar bill is the sign of Illuminati, the secret sect founded in Bavaria in 1776 that's plotting to take over the world.

2. The government controls the weather.

3. The United States government is run by the New World Order, a secret regime out to disarm American citizens and subjugate everyone to a totalitarian world government.

4. The United Nations is a front organization for the New World Order.

5. Markings on the backs of road signs contain coded messages to guide invading United Nations armed forces.

FRIGHT 🐓 BITE!

You are more likely to be struck by lightning than eaten by a shark.

Was that
click a
wiretap?

MOST wiretapping devices emit no audible sounds.

FRIGHT 🐓 BITE!

You are more likely to be infected by flesh-eating bacteria than struck by lightning.

where else. Someone put LSD in the drinking water. Antiperspirants cause can-

Dozens of marketing companies are compiling profiles of you—including your name, address, and occupation—based upon every Web site you've ever visited. If you call **1-800** or **1-900** numbers, your phone number can be captured by automatic number identification (ANI) and added to your consumer profile, which can be bought and traded.

cer. Someone watched me come into my apartment building, so I can't turn on

What are they looking for?

New York City officials claim that alligators no longer live in the city's sewer system, yet the city monitors its 6,200 miles of sewers with TV cameras.

FRIGHT 🐦 BITE!

Lightning strikes the earth 6,000 times every minute.

any lights for 10 minutes or they will know which apartment is mine. Snakes will

THE VAMPIRE RESEARCH CENTER, in Elmhurst, New York, has been thriving since 1972.

Business sucks.

FRIGHT 🦇 BITE!

People forget up to 80% of what they learn within 24 hours.

Infected vampire bats have caused a series of fatal rabies outbreaks among humans. Despite a wingspan of up two feet, the nocturnal creatures are difficult to see at night due to their dark-gray coloring. Their teeth are so sharp they can easily slice a hole in your skin without even waking you. Most vampire bats will drink three-fifths of their own body weight in one sitting, but they don't actually suck blood; they lap it up with their tongue. The tiny hole would shed less than a gram of blood if not for the vampire bat's anticoagulant, known as *plasminogen*, or Bat-PA, which prevents the blood from clotting.

Vampire bats kill humans.

Explosive cap. In July 1996, a Colorado woman's head was engulfed in a ball of flame when she unscrewed the gas tank cap of her car at a service station. She was unhurt, but the flames singed off her eyebrows and eyelashes and most of her hair. The explosion was caused when static electricity transferred from her hand to the gas cap, igniting the fumes inside the tank.

FRIGHT 🦎 BITE!

Fifteen percent of the nation's fatal accidents are caused by the 1% of drivers with revoked or suspended licenses.

In most communities, there is at least a 20% chance that the water supply is not chlorinated sufficiently to kill **_infectious bacteria_** that lead to diseases such as cryptosporidiosis. But if your tap water is chlorinated, and you drink a lot of it, you face an increased risk of bladder cancer.

Just a glass of water.

the subscription label off my magazine and send in a change of address. My

FRIGHT 🐦 BITE!

A man is twice as likely to fall out of a hospital bed as a woman.

You never know until it's too late.

ONE IN THREE MEN OVER AGE 60 WILL SUFFER FROM IMPOTENCE.

hairstylist will have a burst of creative inspiration while cutting my hair. I will

If you urinate when swimming in a South American river, you may encounter the candiru. Drawn to warmth, this tiny fish is known to follow a stream of urine to its source, swim inside the body, and flare its barbed fins. It will remain firmly embedded in the flesh until surgically removed.

The candiru.

FRIGHT 🐦 BITE!

There are at least 18 different ways to tap a telephone.

grow up and have children just like me. People know what I'm thinking. I go

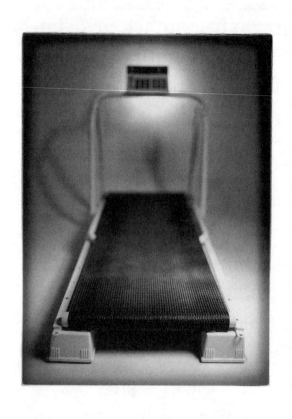

[A TREADMILL]

At the Gym

TREADMILLS.

Each year, thousands of people fall from treadmills that unexpectedly start, stop, or change speeds. A 26-year-old Virginia man broke both legs when he fell off a treadmill that changed speed without warning.

EVERYONE IN THE POOL.

The more people in the swimming pool with you, the higher your chances of ingesting *Cryptosporidium parvum*. Highly resistant to chlorine, this emerging pathogen is transmitted through fecal excrement and causes nausea, abdominal cramps, and acute diarrhea lasting 7 to 14 days.

| At the Gym |

SADDLE SORES SOAR.

Did the guy riding the stationary bike before you leave something on the seat? Perhaps it's *Tinea cruris*, the fungus that causes jock itch and covers the groin area with itchy red patches.

SHOWERS.

A hot, steamy shower after a work-out can be so relaxing—unless the organism that causes Legionnaires' disease is growing inside the showerhead. To contract this deadly disease, all you have to do is inhale steam containing *Legionella pneumophila* bacteria.

KEEP PEDALING.

Every year, close to 200 exercisers fall victim to metal seat posts when the seats on their stationary bikes collapse.

When was the last time you checked the interest rate in the fine print on your credit-card bill? How long is your billing cycle? Do you pay a fee and interest daily for a cash advance? Credit-card issuers can increase their rates and reduce reward programs at any time.

Your rates may vary.

away for two weeks without telling anyone and no one notices I'm gone. The

At the Gym
WORRIES

1. Walking into the wrong locker room.

2. The naked person I'm staring at turns around and it's my boss.

3. Getting turned-on during my massage.

4. Going blind if a drop of hot water falls from the ceiling of the steam room and lands in my eye.

5. Doing one-too-many bench presses and getting pinned under the bar.

At the Gym
WORRIES

6. Walking into a mirror while I'm checking someone out.

7. No one is checking me out.

8. What is that at the bottom of the pool?

9. Farting while stretching.

10. Other people counting how few repetitions I'm doing.

11. Falling down during aerobics class.

Manholes. Liverpool, England, has been plagued by exploding manhole covers since a new sewer ventilation system was installed in 1994. But manhole covers have been exploding for years. In August 1989, gas trapped inside a New York sewer exploded, sending a manhole cover 30 feet into the air and killing two pedestrians. In 1992, a Washington, D.C., man riding his bicycle was lifted high in the air when the manhole he was riding over exploded. In October 1990, an entire People Mover train in Detroit was derailed by an explosion that blew up a number of manhole covers in the area.

bathtub will fall through to the apartment below with me sitting in it naked.

[A MANHOLE COVER]

Micro-scopic assassins. Tiny antimicrobial pellets, designed to kill germs on the spot, are currently being added to a wide range of products, including clothing, bedding, footwear, toys, kitchen products, and toothbrushes.

FRIGHT 🦎 BITE!

There are over 1,100 hazardous-waste sites in the United States. New Jersey has more than any other state.

Flying is a gamble. The first automated teller machines are being installed on airplanes. Not only do they dispense currency and telephone calling cards, they also will be used to facilitate in-flight gambling.

FRIGHT 🦜 BITE!

A divorced man is four times more likely to die in an accident than a married man.

When you pay for your groceries with a credit card, bank debit card, or discount shopping card, data from supermarket scanners can be merged with your financial profile and the information sold to marketers.

Checked

out.

FRIGHT 🦜 BITE!

This year, more than 5,000 people will injure themselves playing pool.

What are they really doing?

The IRS has more employees than the FBI or any other law enforcement agency.

on a Post-it stuck to my butt. I will get cancer from walking through metal detec-

FRIGHT 🐦 BITE!

You are four times more likely to get food poisoning from eating at a restaurant than eating at home.

In your 30s, you will begin to lose neurons in the hippocampus, the part of the brain that converts short-term ideas to long-term memories. By the time you reach your 70s, a third of them will be gone.

Remember this.

FRIGHT 🐦 BITE!

Using a cellular telephone while driving increases your chances of being in an accident by 34%.

tors. The grocery store checker will make me put the ice cream back because

THE SPONGE.

All those moist little holes make your sponge the most germ-infested object in the kitchen. Did you touch your mouth after wiping off the counter? Did you scrub that spoon before or after stirring your coffee? Nearly two-thirds of all kitchen sponges are covered with a variety of bacteria, including deadly salmonella.

CUTTING BOARDS.

Kitchen cutting boards, especially plastic ones, can be a major breeding ground for disease. Contaminated foods, sponges, and airborne microbes transfer dangerous bacteria to the surface, where they can live for days in moist cracks and crevices.

[A SPONGE]

At Home

NICE LAWN.
Most fatal lawn-mower accidents occur when the machine tips over and the victim falls or is thrown from the mower. There are 18,000 other lawn mower injuries per year.

STIRRING UP TROUBLE.
Vacuuming agitates particles in the air such as disease-causing mold, rodent feces, and dust mites. Dust mites are microscopic insects that live on dead skin cells from people and animals, from which they get moisture and food.

SLIPPERY WHEN WET.
Bathroom sinks cause over 45,000 injuries every year.

THE BATHROOM.

After the kitchen, the bathroom is the second-most dangerous room in the house; approximately 200,000 serious injuries happen there each year. The most common bathroom injuries are burns, falls, and electric shocks.

YOUR TOWEL.

When you dry off with a towel, dead skin cells cling to its surface, providing protein to feed microorganisms such as *Staphylococcus aureus*, which can cause infection and pustules. Even the clean towel you used last night will be crawling with organisms by the time you use it this morning.

At Home

NO NIGHT LIGHT.
A major cause of serious injury to overnight guests is mistaking a door leading downstairs for a door to the bathroom.

ALARMING CLOCK.
Electromagnetic rays emitted from alarm clocks are believed to cause cellular mutation and increase the risk of cancer. Most people spend over a third of their life asleep in bed.

BLIND LUCK.
Unless you purchased your mini-blinds after July 1995, it could be curtains for you! Inexpensive plastic miniblinds made before then deteriorate over time, exposing you and your family to poisonous lead dust. Just inhaling or swallowing a tiny amount can cause brain damage.

At Home

UNDERCOVER.

Sleeping under an electric blanket that's on all night can expose you to dangerous levels of electromagnetic radiation, which is believed to increase the risk of cancer.

BED NEWS.

Rest easy, only 130 Americans die from falling out of bed each year. But that doesn't include the 70,000 or so who will be injured by collapsing headboards, buckling frames, or mechanical failure. The most common injury suffered in bed is a heart attack: if you're over 35, you face a 1 in 77 chance of suffering a serious heart attack during sex.

Gas barbecues. When a pilot light in a gas barbecue fails to ignite the gas jets promptly, it is easy for you to inhale gas accidentally while trying to light it by hand. If this has happened, when the match does light, a *trail of flame* will blaze from the jet into your mouth, filling your lungs with fire. Oddly enough, you would suffocate before burning to death as the flame consumes the oxygen in every breath you take.

FRIGHT 🗲 BITE!

During aerobic exercise, only one out of four calories you burn is fat.

I'm too fat. The guy I'm going out with tonight won't call me tomorrow because

FRIGHT 🐦 BITE!

Cold- and warm-water laundry cycles will not kill bacteria and microscopic insects living in your clothes and bedding.

Approximately 2,000 Americans are poisoned to death by motor-vehicle exhaust every year. Most are suicides. Because of higher emission-control standards, it now takes three times longer to poison yourself with carbon monoxide.

I'm

exhausted.

FRIGHT 🐦 BITE!

Eleven unintentional fatal injuries and 2,120 disabling injuries occur during every hour of the year.

---

he thinks I'm ugly / he hates me / his friends hate me / I didn't sleep with him /

Things to Worry About

WHILE DRIVING

1. Did I close the garage door?

2. Is that burning smell coming from my car?

3. What if objects in the mirror are not closer than they appear?

4. What's that rattling sound?

5. Have I filled too much of my memory with stupid song lyrics?

6. Did I mail my bills in the video drop-off box?

7. Have my lug nuts been loosened? Are my wheels about to fall off?

Things to Worry About
WHILE DRIVING

8. Do bugs feel pain when they hit the windshield?

9. Talk radio?

10. If I hit the brakes too hard, will the airbag slap me in the face going 200 miles an hour and crush my nose?

11. Can I take my jacket off before the light changes?

12. If I cut that guy off, will he shoot me?

13. If I open my windows when I'm driving, the exhaust from the other cars will poison me; if I don't open my windows, I'll slowly suffocate.

Unfairly labeled. Have you ever wondered what information is encoded in the jumbled numbers and letters in the top right corner on the mailing label that the IRS expects you to use on your tax return? What does the IRS really do with its computerized national data base, which merges information from your tax returns with data provided by employers, banks, real-estate agents, universities, corporations, car dealers, and other organizations? And, unlike all other federal and state agencies, the IRS has the power to order these entities and institutions to provide information about you without a warrant.

I slept with him / he already has another relationship. If I'm too strict, my kids

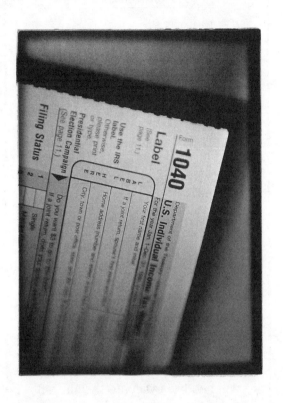

[A TAX FORM]

On a Plane

HEADPHONES.

The soft, plastic headphones used on airplanes create a warm, moist environment in the ear canal that is ideal for breeding bacteria. Wearing headphones for just an hour will increase the bacteria in your ear by 700 times. Could the static you hear while watching an in-flight movie actually be the sound of bacteria rapidly reproducing inside your ear?

WHY IS THE EMERGENCY HANDLE SO BIG?

The odds are better that some stressed-out, claustrophobic passenger will try to open the emergency exit at 39,000 feet than a carefully trained flight attendant will need to evacuate the aircraft during an emergency landing.

On a Plane

GEAR FOR FEAR.

When a plane's hydraulic landing gear fails to drop and lock into place, airport safety crews spray the runway with a thick layer of foam that not only acts as a lubricant but also helps to extinguish the 40- to 50-foot trail of friction flames.

LEAN BACK AND RELAX.

Are you stuck in a middle seat on a long flight? Do you usually take something that knocks you out when you fly? Passengers who don't move around during a flight are much more susceptible to deep-vein thrombosis—blood clots. Lower levels of oxygen and low humidity inside the cabin make blood stickier and more likely to clot. Cardiovascular problems are the number-one cause of death during air travel.

CHEST PAINS.
Pulmonary embolisms occur most often during descent. Drinking coffee or alcohol during a flight puts you in the high-risk category; if you're on birth control, you're also at risk.

STRONG TAILWINDS.
If the passenger in your seat on the incoming flight had serious gas, then you're sitting on a cushion full of disease-causing microbes.

SAFETY FAST.
The people who screen baggage at airport security checkpoints get only eight hours of instruction in the classroom and four hours of on-the-job training. Even so, security guards daily find at least eight Americans attempting to board a plane with a firearm or explosives.

On a Plane

AIRPORT FOOD.
Twenty-nine percent of experienced pilots have become so sick that they couldn't complete a flight. Most had eaten at the airport.

OCCUPIED.
All bathrooms on commercial airplanes can be unlocked from the outside simply by moving a small lever that's in plain sight.

BREATHE EASY.
Every time you hear another passenger cough or sneeze, it's only a matter of time before you inhale their infectious germs, which might range from a cold to tuberculosis. At best, only 50% of the air circulating on newer planes is fresh.

[A PILLOW]

On a Plane

PILLOWS.

Drool. Head lice. Dandruff. Fungus. Why don't more airlines change the pillows or pillowcases between flights?

TOOTHACHES.

Bacteria inside a decaying tooth emit gas. As air pressure changes during a flight, the gas expands, causing an excruciating pain called "tooth squeeze."

SEATBELTS SHOULD BE SECURELY FASTENED.

In 1996, the rear stairway on a flight from St. Louis to San Antonio dropped open at an altitude of 35,000 feet. At a lower altitude, a crew member—tethered by seatbelts—was able to reach out of the opening, grab the lever, and pull the stairway closed.

It's a bird, it's a plane. Some airplane-engine manufacturers test their products by firing chickens from a specially designed cannon to see if the engines are able to digest a bird without malfunctioning. Other manufacturers find out the hard way.

FRIGHT 🦔 BITE!

Seventeen people are electrocuted every year by hair dryers.

It's a gas. Radon seeping from the ground, through foundations, and into homes may be causing lung cancer in as many as 20,000 people every year. This *invisible, odorless,* and *tasteless gas* is present at unsafe levels in over 21% of U.S. households.

When your expensive meal comes out of the restaurant kitchen beauti- fully arranged on the plate, someone's hands have been all over your food.

Finger food.

FABULOUS

Phobias

AMATHOPHOBIA:
the fear of dust.

DECORAPHOBIA:
the fear of interior decorating.

HEORTOPHOBIA:
the fear of holidays.

POGONOPHOBIA:
the fear of beards.

GENUPHOBIA:
the fear of knees.

ARCHIBUTYROPHOBIA:
the fear of peanut butter sticking
to the roof of your mouth.

PHOBOPHOBIA:
the fear of fear itself.

SCOPOPHOBIA:
the fear of being naked.

FABULOUS
Phobias

GEMOPHOBIA:
the fear of prominent chins.

BATRACHOPHOBIA:
the fear of reptiles.

CHOROPHOBIA:
the fear of dancing.

OSPHRESIOPHOBIA:
the fear of body odor.

PHAGOPHOBIA:
the fear of swallowing.

HELMINTHOPHOBIA:
the fear of worms.

ODONTOPHOBIA:
the fear of teeth.

HODOPHOBIA:
the fear of travel.

PARTHENOPHOBIA:
the fear of young girls.

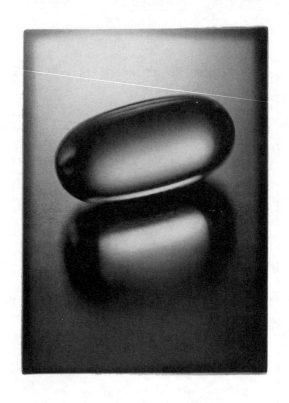

[A PILL]

HYPOCHONDRIAC'S
Alert

*More than one quarter of all patients
who visit doctors complain of symptoms
that appear to have no medical basis.
Adults tend to experience the same
symptoms they saw in their parents.
Here are symptoms you should watch
for:*

HAIR IN THE SINK:
It could be male pattern baldness,
a fungal infection, or a surprisingly
common stress-related disorder
called *alopecia universalis,* which
causes all the hair on your body,
including eyelashes and eyebrows,
to fall out.

CHEST PAINS:
It could be over-exertion, indiges-
tion, or angina signaling a heart
attack.

HYPOCHONDRIAC'S
Alert

EXCESSIVE BLINKING:
It could be dryness of the eyes, a nervous twitch, or an early sign of blepharospasm, a rare muscle disorder that causes the eyelids to lock shut permanently.

BODY ODOR:
It could be time for a new deodorant, a sign of hormonal changes, or the onset of trimethylaminuria (the fish odor syndrome), a persistent and highly offensive body odor that smells of rotting fish. This syndrome is believed to be caused by depression, relationship or career problems, substance abuse, and/or paranoia.

HYPOCHONDRIAC'S
Alert

WRINKLES:
It could be dry skin, sun damage, or the first signs of progeria, the premature-aging disease that makes cells mysteriously stop reproducing, causing gray hair, baldness, and sagging, wrinkled skin within just a few months.

SHORTNESS OF BREATH, CHEST PAINS, AND DIZZINESS:
It could be love, the warning signs of heart disease, or a panic attack—which often causes a heart attack.

SEVERE DIARRHEA:
It could be food poisoning, irritable bowel syndrome, or the Ebola virus, which causes hemorrhaging from every orifice and has a 90% fatality rate.

HYPOCHONDRIAC'S
Alert

HEADACHE AND NAUSEA:
It could be a hangover, the flu, or mad cow disease, which quickly destroys the central nervous system and transforms the brain into a spongy mass.

STOMACH PAIN:
It could be gas, a peptic ulcer, or a parasite digging into the wall of your stomach.

HEADACHE:
It could be tension, eyestrain, a migraine, meningitis, or a brain tumor.

SORE THROAT:
It could be a common cold, strep throat, or an early sign of chronic fatigue syndrome.

HYPOCHONDRIAC'S
Alert

DARK SPOTS:
It could be a new mole, an age spot, or a malignant melanoma.

MEMORY PROBLEMS:
It could be chronic fatigue syndrome, cerebral arteriosclerosis, Alzheimer's disease, or—uh—something else.

INCONTINENCE:
It could be inattention, a bladder infection, diabetes, or bladder cancer.

ANXIETY ATTACKS:
It could be too much caffeine, an overactive thyroid gland, or post-traumatic stress disorder (PTSD).

HYPOCHONDRIAC'S
Alert

WORM CRAWLING ACROSS THE
SURFACE OF YOUR EYEBALL:
It could be that you've had too
much mescal or that you've been
bitten by a large chrysops fly
infected with what's known as the
African eye worm.

ITCHY SKIN:
It could be a spider bite, the first
sign of herpes, or Streptococcus-
A, flesh-eating bacteria that
destroys tissue so quickly it can kill
you in days.

PIMPLES:
It could be acne, sebaceous cysts,
or boils caused by mphutsi fly mag-
gots that have burrowed under
your skin.

Illnesses caused by poor ventilation in office buildings have become so common that they have a special name—"sick-office syndrome." Nearly a third of all commercial office buildings in the United States have serious problems with indoor air quality that can expose workers to chemical fumes as well as increase the risk of transmitting airborne diseases. In Pontiac, Michigan, 95% of the people working in the County Health Department contracted *Legionella pneumophila.* Now known as Pontiac fever, this flu-like illness is transmitted by the same organism that causes Legionnaires' disease. The source of the outbreak proved to be the building's air-conditioning system.

Clearing the air.

FRIGHT 🦜 BITE!
Fleas can jump 13 feet from a standing position.

of every petition I've ever signed. I will show up at a party wearing the same

Wear a bell when ice fishing.

Polar Bears can smell humans 20 miles away. They run at speeds up to 25 miles per hour and can outswim any human, even an Olympic record-holder.

FRIGHT 🐓 BITE!

Thirty-four percent of hunting deaths and injuries are self-inflicted.

Hold my calls.

In 1994, electromagnetic interference (EMI) from a nearby cellular telephone activated a power wheelchair at a scenic vista in Colorado, **SENDING THE PASSENGER OVER A CLIFF**. EMI from computers, radios, and TVs, as well as cell phones, has also caused ventilators, defibrillators, electro-cardiogram monitors, baby incubators, infusion pumps, and blood warmers to malfunction without warning.

outfit my stepmother is wearing. Plucking nose hairs will cause a brain aneurysm.

If you're going to be murdered, it's more like-ly to happen on January 1 than on any other day.

Who's your date for New Year's Eve?

I'll never be able to afford getting my clothes back from the dry cleaner. My ther-

[A HAND]

Hands Off

Take a good look at your hands. They're crawling with bacteria, microorganisms, and viruses that can lead to disease. No matter how often or vigorously you wash your hands, it's impossible to sterilize them. Bacteria love to hide between fingers, around cuticles, and under nails and rings. Worse yet, every time you touch a bar of soap, a faucet handle, or a bathroom doorknob, you pick up more germs. Beware of people with clammy hands—bacteria thrive on warm, moist surfaces.

WHAT'S GROWING ON YOUR HAND?

1. *Rhinovirus* (can cause a cold)

2. *Andenovirus* (may cause conjunctivitis and other eye infections)

3. *Shingella* (can cause cramps and bloody diarrhea)

4. *Staphylococcus aureus* (may cause local infections, such as pimples, boils, and sties)

5. *Pseudomonas aeruginosa* (can produce a blue-green pus)

6. *Haemophilus influenza* (can cause ear infections or meningitis)

7. Hepatitis-A virus

Video cameras don't actually reduce crime, but they do motivate criminals to move to other neighborhoods.

Security camera.

apist is crazier than I am. Someone will have a heart attack right in front of me,

Ten common breeding
GROUNDS FOR DISEASE

doorknobs

elevator buttons

handrails

automated teller machines

computer keyboard and mouse

change-machine bins

light switches

water-faucet handles

telephone receivers

the pen you're sucking on

[A PUBLIC PHONE]

MORE POPULAR BREEDING GROUNDS
for Disease

Restaurant menus

Hospital beds

Palms of toll-booth collectors

Handkerchiefs

Drinking fountains

Parking meters

Shopping-cart handles

Self-service coffeepots

Bars and counters

Money

Homely criminals get 50% longer jail sentences than good-looking criminals.

If you're ugly, don't get caught.

FRIGHT 🐦 BITE!

You can be electrocuted while talking on the telephone during a thunderstorm.

A 22-year-old man was trapped against the wall of a swimming pool when his penis became stuck in a suction hole. The pool's pump had to be turned off in order to free the man.

The hole story.

FRIGHT 🐦 BITE!

The chance of contracting an infection during a stay in a hospital in the United States is 1 in 15.

and I'll completely forget CPR. I will get stuck on an airplane suction toilet when

U.S. law bans flying saucer rides with extra-terrestrials.

If the government has no knowledge of **ALIENS**, then why does Title 14, Section 1211 of the Code of Federal Regulations, implemented on July 16, 1969, make it illegal for U.S. citizens to have any contact with extraterrestrials or their vehicles?

FRIGHT BITE!

A sinkhole can open up and consume a person, a car, or even a house in a matter of seconds.

Shaky fingers on the button.

Approximately 23,000 American nuclear warheads are armed and ready in silos, bases, and submarines around the world. After finding dozens of military personnel in key nuclear weaponry positions who were psychologically unfit, the U.S. Navy elected to review its program designed to prevent unstable individuals from obtaining access to nuclear weapons.

I flush. If I spill bleach on my hand, all of my skin will burn off. I will unex-

FRIGHT 🦔 BITE!

Approximately 30 times as many people die in natural disasters each year as in man-made disasters.

It's not the taste of your blood that attracts mosquitoes to you—it's your own special body odor caused by bacteria growing on the skin.

What's that buzzing?

FRIGHT 🦔 BITE!

More people working in advertising died on the job last year than died while working in petroleum refining.

pectedly end up in bed with someone I'm really attracted to and discover that

Lost nuclear sub-marines. Four sunken nuclear submarines sit at the bottom of the Atlantic Ocean. One, a Russian sub resting in deep waters off the island of Bermuda, holds 16 live nuclear warheads. Scientists and oceanographers are unsure what impact the escaping plutonium will have but warn that corrosion may lead to a massive nuclear chain reaction.

FRIGHT 🦔 BITE!

Air inside parking garages contains dangerous levels of toxins from automobile emissions that are known to cause cancer and birth defects.

I'm wearing my last clean pair of underwear, which is too small, filled with holes,

FRIGHT 🦜 BITE!

In 1996, the Centers for Disease Control reported that it does not have a large enough budget to research all of the emerging pathogens.

A memo written in July 1969 refers to the formation of an internal unit to oversee all IRS monitoring of "ideological, militant, subversive, radical, and similar type organizations." This group was known as the Special Service Staff.

Tax service.

FRIGHT 🦜 BITE!

Over 30,000 people are seriously injured by exercise equipment each year.

Stress causes a host of unhealthy physiological changes, including high blood pressure, muscle tension, and immuno-suppression.

Don't worry about your health.

and tie-dyed. The day after I write out a will, I'll die. I think it's Friday when it's

*How long
is long
enough?*

Women are more sexually attracted to men with a **LONG** stride.

really only Thursday and I am the only person at work wearing shorts. If I have

A man is much more likely to help an attractive woman who is bleeding than an injured homely woman.

Insult to injury.

FRIGHT 🦔 BITE!

An unusually long yawn can break your jawbone.

It's much harder to tell a *convincing lie* to someone you're physically attracted to.

"Of course I'll respect you in the morning."

FRIGHT 🦔 BITE!

A serious earthquake causing over 1,000 fatalities occurs about once a year.

a one-night stand, the condom will break, she'll get pregnant, and want to keep

DO YOU THINK I'M SEXY?
Adults are more likely to tell a lie
in bed than anywhere else.

HONEY, I DON'T EVEN LOOK
AT ANYONE BUT YOU.
One in three men cheat on their
partners. One in four women
cheat.

OH BABY, YOU'RE THE ONE.
Most men can't remember the
names of all their sex partners.
One in four women can't remember the names of all of their lovers.

Sex and Dating

WAS IT GOOD FOR YOU?
Most straight men have no idea when their partner is having an orgasm.

PRIVATE DICKS.
Did you tell your girlfriend a little white lie about what you do for a living and how much you make? Did you say those three years were spent in grad school when you meant to say prison? Or maybe you just forgot to tell her that your divorce isn't quite final. Women hire private investigators more often than men to see if the person they are dating is really marriage material.

Sex and Dating

ARE YOUR DATES ALWAYS
GETTING PAGED IN THE
MIDDLE OF DINNER?
Maybe it's because you're so bor-
ing! Phoney pagers are activated
by the person wearing them.
There's no way to tell by looking if
a pager is real or a fake.

NOT SAFE ENOUGH.

1. If a woman is on the pill, there
   is still a 5% chance she'll get
   pregnant.

2. When used correctly, dia-
   phragms don't work 3%
   to 18% of the time.

3. Even if a condom is brand
   new, there is a 5% to 15%
   chance you'll be changing
   diapers in a year.

[CONTRACEPTION]

FRIGHT 🐦 BITE!

Bee stings cause three to four times more deaths than snake-bites.

In May 1993, the U.S. Army's monthly journal *Military Review,* which is circulated to nearly 20,000 senior officers, published an article entitled, "Hell in a Handbasket: The Threat of Portable Nuclear Weapons." According to the *New York Times,* the author of the article, who described himself as "a freelance researcher for the Pentagon and the U.S. Department of Energy," was in a mental institution at the time.

FRIGHT 🐦 BITE!

Don't worry about being short; anxiety stunts growth.

Psychologists now recognize a new neurosis known as "tan obsessed," a condition with serious health consequences. Compulsive tanners constantly think and talk about their tans and organize their lives around tanning opportunities. When unable to tan, or if they think their tan is fading, they become highly distressed.

Nice tan.

late that I didn't lock the bathroom door. I will be left at the altar. I will pass

Patched up. A Milwaukee man experienced violent nausea and severe headaches for three days before an emergency-room resident found the cause of illness—his wife's estrogen patch was stuck to the back of his thigh.

FRIGHT 🐦 BITE!

Half of this year's college seniors will still be jobless a year after they graduate.

Crisis misman- agement. According to a Pentagon official, half of the initial internal reporting within the government during a crisis is wrong.

FRIGHT 🐦 BITE!

As large oceangoing ships travel from port to port, they carry bacteria in their ballast water that spreads cholera and other deadly diseases.

gas when alone in an elevator and someone will get in before I can get out. My

VERY ATTRACTIVE MEN AND WOMEN earn at least 5% more per hour than people with average looks. Plain women earn 5% less than women with average looks, and plain men earn 10% less than average men. Most employers pay *overweight* women 20% less an hour than women of average weight, while men who are slightly *overweight* earn 26% more than their *underweight* coworkers. Of men with virtually identical resumés, the taller man will be hired about 72% of the time. Men who are 6'2" or taller receive starting salaries 12% higher than men under six feet.

Not getting ahead?

barber is nodding and smiling because he doesn't speak English and has no

Runaway satellites. A runaway satellite weighing about two tons would impact the Earth at a speed of 200 to 400 mph and cause an explosion big enough to destroy a three-bedroom house. Most comprehensive home and auto insurance policies offer coverage for destruction by satellite.

Misting systems in the produce department at your local grocery store may be doing more than hydrating vegetables. They could be spreading bacteria that cause deadly Legionnaires' disease. *Legionella pneumophila* bacteria has been found rapidly multiplying inside wet spray nozzles, just inches from produce and shoppers' lungs.

Fresh produce.

skinny because I have a tapeworm, and I've had it all my life. There's something

Smile while you can. A simple collagen injection can trigger an autoimmune disease called PM/DM that leads to **MASSIVE SWELLING**, redness, boils, partial paralysis, bladder failure, and even death.

FRIGHT 🐭 BITE!

Seventy percent of both men and women fantasize about someone else while making love.

UFOs. A recent study indicates that well-educated men who are frustrated in their work are many times more likely to report UFO sightings than men who are more successful.

One in three adults suffers from insomnia, which often is a symptom of mental illness.

Having trouble sleeping again?

for 30 years. I will drop the baby on his head. I'll be caught in the shower dur-

Pet window. Does your pet love to sit on the windowsill and watch the world go by? It may be on the verge of succumbing to "high-rise cat syndrome." An alarming number of urban pets—cats, dogs, and reptiles—inexplicably jump from urban high-rises every summer. Many actually land on their feet and survive. A New York University study determined that plummeting pets gather a terminal velocity of 60 miles an hour after five stories.

ing a major earthquake. The phone will stop ringing when I get inside the front

FRIGHT 🐦 BITE!

More than 8,000 computer viruses are thriving worldwide, and three to six new ones are created every day. The main way viruses spread is through the Internet.

SURVEYS SHOW THAT AFTER THE HONEYMOON IS OVER, THE NEXT PERIOD OF MARITAL BLISS OCCURS ABOUT 30 YEARS LATER—WHEN THE KIDS ARE OUT OF THE HOUSE AND YOU'RE CLOSE TO RETIREMENT.

Happily married?

door. The bank is siphoning money from my account. I'll get a disease that no

Are you a really hot dancer?

Dance-floor dehydration syndrome can kill you.

FRIGHT 🐦 BITE!

Heading a soccer ball frequently (10 or more times per game) causes mild neuropsychological damage and lowers IQ.

It's only a matter of time.

There are 120 major terrestrial impact craters on the surface of the Earth. Over 2,000 known asteroids are intersecting with the Earth's orbit.

one has ever had before, and every doctor I see will think I'm just a hypochon-

Do you belong to an **HMO**? Then your doctor may not be telling you everything about your condition. A growing number of managed health-care operators require doctors to discuss treatment options and referrals with the insurer before they can talk to their patients.

Who's getting better treat-ment?

In September 1996, a London-based insurance company introduced a policy that pays $333,000 if the insured party becomes impregnated by aliens.

Universal coverage.

driac. The hood on my car will fly off and smash the windshield. If I squeeze a

Sorry, wrong number.

Have you ever called the IRS to ask a question when preparing your tax returns? One out of three answers they provide is wrong or incomplete.

FRIGHT BITE!

According to the Federal Aviation Administration, 13% of the commercial airline pilots tested positive for alcohol or drugs while on duty.

Garbanzo beans stink.

In Minneapolis, a 34-year-old man who suffered from severe food allergies succumbed to an allergic reaction triggered by the smell of garbanzo beans cooking in a neighbor's apartment.

pimple above eyebrow level, I'll get permanent brain damage. The tickets will

In 1996, the U.S. Army planned to destroy over 14,000 tons of chemical weapons by burning them in a specially designed incinerator in a remote area of Utah. After operating for three days, the incinerator was shut down because it was leaking nerve gas.

Passing gas.

be sold out when I get there. My neighbors will see my recycling and think I'm

WHICH CAME FIRST, THE SALMONELLA OR THE EGG?

A new type of *Salmonella* bacteria, called *Salmonella enteritidis,* has been discovered living inside raw eggs. Eating raw or under-cooked eggs can lead to severe food poisoning and even death. Eating anything made with raw eggs—homemade ice cream, egg-nog, hollandaise sauce, French toast, smoothies, Caesar salad—also puts you at risk.

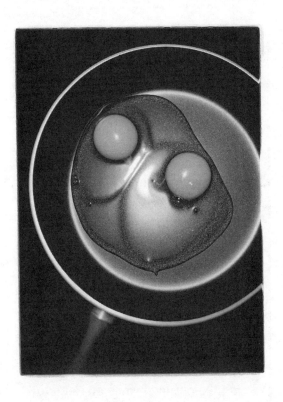

[E G G S]

Food

FOOD CHAIN.

Roughly 50% of all commercially raised chickens and turkeys succumb to *Salmonella* poisoning every year. More than a billion pounds of dead poultry are recycled annually into poultry feed. About 90% of all food-borne illnesses can be transmitted from animals to humans. Many *Salmonella* strains have become resistant to antibiotics.

HOW LONG WILL IT TAKE?

How far is your house from the restaurant? How many stops did the delivery guy make before yours? Did he visit his girlfriend on the way? It takes only a few minutes for harmful bacteria to grow in take-out food while en route to your door.

Food

SUSHI.

The best sushi chefs know to check raw salmon or red snapper for worms by holding thin cuts of fish up to a light. But for some reason, anisakis, a disease caused by ingesting worms in raw fish, is on the rise. Up to 80% of certain species caught off the Pacific Coast may be infected with this fish parasite. If you eat one, you'll know. A day or two later, you'll feel a burning sensation in your gut as the parasite bores through the stomach lining.

OF COURSE THE CHEF WASHES HIS HANDS.

Eleven percent of all restaurant dishcloths are contaminated with *L. monocytogenes*.

Food

VEGGIE ALERT:

1. Now *Salmonella* bacteria live on alfalfa sprouts.

2. *E. coli* bacteria are able to thrive on iceberg lettuce.

3. Packaging used for mushrooms incubates highly evolved spores and toxins such as *C. boulinum*.

MUTATING BACTERIA.
In the last 20 years, scientists have identified over 25 new microbes that cause deadly food-borne illnesses.

As the baby-boomer generation ages, more women than ever before will be in the prime of menopause at the same time. In the year 2000, approximately 19 million women will be suffering anxiety, insomnia, irritability, and violent mood swings.

Hot flash.

FRIGHT 🐦 BITE!

Some organically grown vegetables, particularly broccoli, can be harmful to infants. Because these plants are grown without pesticides, they produce their own pest-averting toxins.

Nearly 25% of psychologists, psychiatrists, social workers, and other mental health professionals have sexual contact with their patients, many citing "client welfare" as the reason.

Therapy.

a drunk. The hotel hasn't washed the blankets all year. I'll see my gynecologist

[LIPS]

Two-thirds of the people with **HERPES** show no symptoms.

How many people do you kiss in a year?

Organized health care. In August 1996, members of the Genovese organized crime family were charged with infiltrating health maintenance organizations in five states and increasing fees for more than a million customers.

FRIGHT BITE!

Many of the world's major cities contain as many rats as people.

Money laundering. Mitsubishi Bank in Tokyo has opened a totally germ-free branch featuring automated teller machines that are covered in antibacterial plastic and dispense only disinfected cash.

a list of all the library books I've checked out and the videos I've rented. My

Four Minnesota farmers were overcome by poisonous gases after landing in a large manure pit. The first man fell in and the other three jumped in thinking they could rescue one another. All four suffocated from a lethal combination of methane, hydrogen sulfide, carbon dioxide, and ammonia generated by the decomposing manure.

Manure fumes.

house will rotate on its foundation in the night. I will be allergic to something I

Any nut can hunt you down.

Did you accidentally cut someone off on the freeway last week? Maybe that's who's been calling at four in the morning or putting dead rats your mailbox. If someone has your license plate number, with just three phone calls or a modem and Internet access they can get your driver's license number, name, home address, birth date, physical description, and even your Social Security number.

FRIGHT 🦇 BITE!

Saliva is a steady source of nutrients to microorganisms living inside a telephone mouthpiece.

A rancher hoping to cure his rheumatism was cooked to death when he fell asleep in a hot mud bath in Calistoga, California.

Mud pie.

FRIGHT 🐦 BITE!

The bacteria growing in your mouth produce proteins that eat away your teeth.

Is it just a coincidence that Raytheon Co., which makes Amana home appliances, recently bought E-Systems, Inc., the secretive Dallas-based company that builds much of the military's spy equipment?

Big Brother is cooking.

The ups and downs of implants.

Among the risks of penile implants are infection, which can lead to gangrene and amputation, and migration of the implant device to another part of the body.

FRIGHT 🦜 BITE!

There is a bomb threat made to an American aircraft once a day.

that is slowly cooking my brain. I'll die when my house is a mess and I'll be

An article in the *Journal of Clinical Psychiatry* concluded that compulsive buying should be diagnosed as a mental disorder.

Shopping sickness.

FRIGHT 🐦 BITE!

Department stores now release scents into the air that make a person feel good and want to buy.

Internet infidelity is rampant as married men and women have sexually explicit exchanges with on-line cyberlovers. It's ten o'clock; do you know where your spouse is?

Safe sex or grounds for divorce?

FRIGHT 🐦 BITE!

A wounded or scared yellow jacket emits a high-frequency sound wave that signals other yellow jackets to attack.

remembered forever as an inadequate homemaker. The person I'm dating will

[A TOOTHBRUSH]

One out of 15 people suffers from hepatitis C, a blood-borne virus that kills up to 20% of those infected. You can get it from sharing a toothbrush.

Do your gums ever bleed when you brush?

stop calling me because my belly button is too big. I'll set off the airport metal

Killer belch.

In August 1984, Lake Monoun, in the African nation of Cameroon, suddenly belched a deadly cloud of carbon dioxide gas that killed 37 people. Scientists believe the deadly gas emission was caused when an earthquake, landslide, or strong winds upset the delicate balance of the lake, which is fed by carbonated groundwater. Experts considered the event to be an isolated freak of nature—until it happened two years later at nearby Lake Nyos, asphyxiating more than 1,700 people.

FRIGHT 🦜 BITE!

Hackers infiltrate Pentagon computers more than 160,000 times a year. Roughly 65% succeed on their first try.

Watching from above.

CIA spy satellites are equipped with 20 different types of sensors that are so powerful the government can identify you in your backyard, see if you're barbecuing chicken or steak, and hear how you like it cooked.

detector with my underwire bra. I will get my finger stuck in the drain at the bot-

In the June 1992 issue of the *Journal of Medical Ethics*, a clinical psychologist proposed that happiness be classified as a psychiatric disorder, arguing that happy people suffer from impaired judgment that prevents them from acquiring a realistic understanding of their physical and social environment.

A cure for happiness.

tom of the pool and drown while everyone watches, thinking that I'm holding

Index

my breath. I suggest to a date that we go out to a tapas bar, but he hears top-

Index

less bar. If I lean back in a movie theater, I'll catch some scalp disease and all

Index

I'll meet my future spouse at a "Learn to Flirt!" adult education class and, for

Index

Index

receive is being delivered to other people. I'll catch my skirt in my pantyhose

Index

and walk around with my underwear showing. Everyone else on the airplane

ABOUT THE
AUTHOR:

Cameron Tuttle is a nervous wreck. She has published many articles on lifestyle trends, entertainment, and fashion, and was the writer of the book *A Brief History of Shorts: The Ultimate Guide to Understanding Your Underwear,* by Joe Boxer. A California native, she developed her theory of niche-worrying while living in New York City. She does not want anyone to know where she lives now, but she can be reached at nervous@aware-house.com.

melon before me. It wasn't really decaf.